*Talk it over with
the Father, then leave the
outcome to His wisdom.*

CATHERINE MARSHALL

The

WOMEN
of FAITH

Prayer

Journal

❖ LANA BATEMAN ❖

COUNTRYMAN ®

Nashville, Tennessee

Prayer is God's
provision for us to know Him,
to know His purposes and
His ways, to experience His
mighty presence working in us
and through us to accomplish
His perfect will.

HENRY BLACKABY

Call to Me, and I will answer you, and I will tell you great and mighty things, which you do not know.

JEREMIAH 33:3 (NAS)

❀ Introduction ❀

A prayer journal is a place to chronicle our times with the Father. Perhaps the most important reason to keep such a record is to encourage our hearts and to remind us of His unfailing love and faithfulness.

When I first started a prayer journal, I wanted only to make note of the ways the Lord might speak to me, but He quickly showed me there was much more to be derived from keeping my prayers on paper.

First, He wanted me to know beyond a doubt that He was the One speaking; the words in my journal were not my words at all. As time passed and I reread the words written, I certainly did see that the Lord had spoken, because I would never have said such words of love and kindness to myself.

Second, as I read the passages over and over again my faith was lifted, and I found fresh encouragement. It didn't matter how much time had passed, the words spoke to me again in that very moment when I re-read them.

Third, I was thrilled to be reminded of the Father's answers to my prayers, and I needed to recall the day-by-day responses that were a part of our times together.

So, dear friend, keep your journal as a precious treasure. It will be a source of comfort, love, and encouragement throughout the years to come. Our times of prayer are worth remembering, for it is in prayer that we meet our Lord in the most intimate of ways.

This is a guided journal. My desire is to walk alongside you through forty days of intimate prayer and then release you into a deeper, richer, ongoing prayer life. On each of the forty days I have listed simple exercises for you to consider as a part of your prayer and devotional time.

May your time with Him through this journal be a life–changing experience and cause you to know your Lord in a fresh and powerful way. Remember, He yearns for you to pray, and He is waiting for you to hear and respond to His heart.

Welcome, my friends! Welcome to His heart of prayer.

Remember . . .

Prayer begins with heart–cleansing and worship. Take time to ask God's forgiveness for the ways you fall short of His great love for you. Then love Him through your worship before moving into your requests and your conversational prayer time. Worship can be anything from singing a simple song of love to Him, to playing and singing worship music, to waving hand banners, or simply telling Him why you love Him.

Here are some other suggestions for making your prayer times more meaningful:

1. Note the dates of your prayers and their answers. This will help you create not just a personal journal, but a history of His responses to your requests.

2. Record any verses, phrases, or song lyrics that come to mind as you spend time with the Lord.

3. When you engage in conversational prayer with your Lord, *expect* Him to respond. Start His response by writing the words, "My Child," at the beginning of your listening time. Trust that He is speaking. When you read back over those things He has impressed on your spirit, you will know it is the Lord.

4. Believe that God desires to communicate with you and don't let the old, "Oh, God isn't interested in me" creep in and rob you of His words to you.

5. Feel free to use a spiral notebook or any other means to give you added space for your chronicling of prayer time.

Knowing His Voice

Here is your test for determining if God is speaking to you.

1. What God speaks *always* edifies His child. His words will build you up, encourage you, show you something you need to see in yourself, or teach you forgiveness.

2. What God speaks *always* is spoken out of love and will produce love.

3. *Nothing* God speaks or asks will contradict or violate Scripture (His revealed Word) in any way. The more you study Scripture, the more you'll recognize when He's speaking . . . or when a counterfeit is speaking.

An understanding of God's sovereignty is pivotal to entering the simplicity of prayer. How can we come to know the *rest* that exists in conversing with our Father if we do not grasp that He is in control of all things?

Christ understood that the Father is always after the highest good. Therefore, no matter what the cost, how unjust, how cruel, or how unfair it might appear, Jesus wanted the Father's will above His own. The Son of God could pray "Thy will be done" because He knew the Father controlled all things.

. . . We should live each day fully as a part of the journey He has given us. One of the great gifts that comes through resting in God's sovereignty is a new heart–set. For when we see that He controls all things, every situation is an opportunity to look for what God has invested in that moment or in that struggle.

—from *The Heart of Prayer*, chapter 1

DAY ONE

*How can we come to know the peace and rest
that exist in conversing with our Father if we do
not grasp that He is in control of all things?*

Describe your understanding of the sovereignty of God.

*That He is almighty and there shall
be no others idols before him or to
replace him.*

How does this influence how you currently respond to God?

*I know that all things occur thru
Christ and that I must be obedient
in His Word and in His Image.*

How does your understanding of God's sovereignty fit into the world's
turmoil today?

*I think the world is going against God's
word and that most people really
don't practice His word although claiming
to be Christian/religious.*

How does it fit into your turmoil?

I must have faith to believe in God and if I ask He shall grant my wishes. I call on God to fight my battles and to give me strength and grace to get thru tribulation

Does God's sovereignty make a difference in your anxiety level? In your confidence level? In your control issues?

Yes it does – Praise Him. I'm learning to let go of my worldly ways and to just trust in the Lord. He is almighty and the Ruler of my life.

Before you pray today, list three ways you see God's sovereignty in your daily life.

1. *In how I treat people. I'm trying to reach out more and to be more loving.*

2. *In my worry. When I have thoughts of worry – I shake them out and ask God to take over.*

3. *In my marriage. I no longer want to be a worldly wife, I want to be a Christian wife and love my husband unconditionally*

> . . . I am the LORD, there is no other,
>
> The one forming light and creating darkness,
>
> Causing well–being and creating calamity;
>
> I am the LORD who does all of these.

ISAIAH 45:6, 7 (NAS)

A Personal Prayer

Date: 7/10/05　　　Time: 5:31 P.m (Sunday)

Dear Lord — thank you for allowing me to witness your beauty another day. I ask that you forgive me Lord if I've fallen in sin and was not living any portion of my life in your image. I love You, Lord and want to live my life according to your word. I worship You for all that You have seen me through, especially in my marriage and I pray that you continue to bless me in Your glory, Lord. I praise You and love You and thank You for Your abundant blessings Lord and I pray that you continue to watch over me and all those whom I love. You are an awesome God.

God never said He would stop the sin that mankind chose.
However, He did promise to be with us through the trials
and difficulties that sin brings forth in our lives.

After your time of worship today, meditate on how God's presence was with you during some of the most painful circumstances in your life.

List three ways that God was with you when others sinned against you.

1. *My teen years were the most traumatic that I can remember.*

2. *When my brother died God gave me strength*

3. *Most of my life – God watched over me and showed me favor when no one else was around.* *I didn't* *I didn't deserve it*

List three ways you "became aware" of God's presence even when you sinned.

1. _____

At this moment nothing comes to mind

2. _____

3. _____

List three events in your life when you did not recognize God's sovereign hand in control.

1. _All of my teen and young adult years._

2. _____

3. _____

As you look back, how do you now see that He was in control all the time?

Because I could not have survived
without His merciful around me.

_____

_____

_____

_____

As you pray today, ask the Lord to reveal to you His presence even in those situations where previously you have not been able to see Him. Meditate on the issues that surrounded those incidents and look for His hand there.

Where can I go from Your Spirit?
Or where can I flee from Your presence?
If I ascend into heaven, You are there;
If I make my bed in hell, behold: You are there.
If I take the wings of the morning,
And dwell in the uttermost parts of the sea,
even there Your hand will lead me . . .

PSALM 139:7–10 (NKJV)

A Personal Prayer

Date: _____ Time: _____

_____

_____

_____

_____

_____

_____

_____

_____

_____

_____

_____

_____

_____

_____

_____

DAY THREE

One of the great gifts that comes through resting in God's sovereignty is a new heart–set. When we see that He controls all things, every situation becomes an opportunity to discover what God has invested in that very moment or in that struggle.

Meditate today on the peace that the sovereignty of God can bring to your heart as you see Him in control of all things.

List three situations where you couldn't let go until you realized God really was in control.

1. *My struggle to quit smoking*

2. *Ending my marriage*

3. *Struggling to live a worldly life while simultaneously living a spiritual life*

Describe your state of mind when you were able to lay down your need to control and lay hold of God's sovereign control.

I was at my wit's end, feeling defeated and unable to defend myself. I felt that God's favor was there to protect me and that I needed to surrender my struggles to God to battle because I could not win on my own.

List three things that keep you from resting in God's sovereignty.

1. _____

_____

2. _____

_____

3. _____

_____

Today in your prayer time, ask God to reveal His sovereignty to you in ways you have not recognized before. Ask Him to help you see that everything rests with Him. Ask Him to bring you to the place where you see His hand in every situation. Explain how you think resting in God's sovereignty might change your life.

_____

_____

_____

Be sure to write down any special ways God directs you to pray and any way in which He speaks to your spirit.

_____

_____

_____

A man's heart plans his way,

But the LORD directs his steps

PROVERBS 16:9 (*NKJV*)

A Personal Prayer

Date: _____ Time: _____

_____

_____

_____

_____

_____

_____

_____

_____

_____

_____

_____

_____

_____

_____

_____

_____

_____

After building a prayer foundation

by understanding God's sovereignty,

we must commit that we will always,

always come to Him honestly in our

prayer times. He is not interested

in pretense or denial. He is

searching for honest hearts.

from *The Heart of Prayer*, chapter 1

Honesty in prayer is critical. It opens the way for us to hear and respond to our Father in deeper and more profound ways. We must purpose in our heart to be open, honest, and transparent, resting in the sovereignty of God. Such a foundation for prayer will never leave us disappointed.

List three areas where you might not have been completely honest with God about situations in your life.

1. _____

_____

2. _____

_____

3. _____

_____

Describe how you have rationalized that "because He already knows" then you "don't need to bring it up" with Him in prayer.

_____

_____

_____

_____

_____

After boldly and honestly bringing the matter before Him, describe how you feel and how you believe your honesty may affect your relationship with the Lord.

_____

_____

_____

Is there now a sense of release in your heart? After your prayer time, explain the difference you discern in your closeness to the Lord.

_____

_____

_____

It is important for you to record the ways you feel God calling you to worship and pray, as well as what He may speak to your spirit during your conversational prayer times.

LORD, who may dwell in Your sanctuary?
Who may live on Your holy hill?
He whose walk is blameless
and who does what is righteous,
who speaks the truth from his heart.

PSALM 15:1, 2 _(NIV)_

A Personal Prayer

Date: _____ Time: _____

_____

_____

_____

_____

_____

_____

_____

_____

_____

_____

_____

_____

_____

_____

_____

_____

_____

Because God inhabits the praises of His people (Psalm 22:3), few things draw Him nearer than our praise and worship. God delights in teaching us different ways of worshiping Him so that our times together are filled with His creative touch. Worship comes before prayer, for it is worship that creates a profound connection between the two of us, better enabling the heart to pray the will of the Father.

"What kind of worship?" you might ask. I quickly found that there are a number of answers to that question. On different days, He led me in different ways. Everything was new. The old habits were gone and now I sat before Him asking what would please Him rather than simply presenting to Him what I felt I should do.

—from *The Heart of Prayer*, chapter 2

DAY FIVE

One of the first steps toward a new and creative experience in prayer is to throw away all of the "shoulds" and "ought-tos" that keep you rigid in times of devotion.

Describe how you feel uneasy about releasing the habits of praying that you have depended upon for years. The Lord wants to hear your concerns.

_____

_____

_____

_____

_____

What will be the greatest hindrance for you in embracing new ways to pray and have devotional times?

_____

_____

_____

_____

_____

List three new things you would like to experience in your personal prayer.

1. _____

_____

2. _____

_____

3. _____

_____

After you worship and pray today, describe how you responded to your new way of coming into the Lord's presence for prayer and devotion.

_____

_____

_____

Tell the Lord of your desire to truly abandon yourself to whatever creative way He may desire to come to you in the future.

_____

_____

_____

I will instruct you and teach you in the way you
should go; I will guide you with My eye.

PSALM 32:8 (*NKJV*)

A Personal Prayer

Date: _____ Time: _____

DAY SIX

Because every good thing comes from God and returns to God,
then even our worship and prayers need to originate with Him.
Our time with Him might begin with, "Lord, how would
You like for me to worship You today, and
how would You like for me to pray?"

Take a moment to acknowledge to the Lord that all good things come from Him and return to Him, therefore good worship and good prayer must be initiated by Him. Confess that you have not realized the importance of asking Him how He would like to be worshiped or how He would like for you to pray each day.

_____

_____

_____

_____

After your prayer time, list the ways He asked you to worship Him today.

_____

_____

_____

_____

List three ways He has asked you to pray over different issues (ways you believe you wouldn't have thought of yourself).

1. _____

_____

2. _____

_____

3. _____

_____

At the end of your prayer time, describe your response to what has transpired between you and the Lord today.

_____

_____

_____

As God speaks to your spirit, write down what is coming through your thoughts. It is important to keep a good record of the prayer times when you especially listen for His voice.

Every good gift and every perfect gift is from above, and comes down from the Father of lights with whom there is no variation or shadow of turning.

JAMES 1:17 (NKJV)

A Personal Prayer

Date: _____ Time: _____

_____
_____
_____
_____
_____
_____
_____
_____
_____
_____
_____
_____
_____
_____
_____
_____
_____
_____
_____

DAY SEVEN

Worship must come before prayer, because worship creates a profound connection between God and the worshiper. This better enables the heart to pray the will of the Father.

Describe your response to your worship experience today.

_____

_____

_____

Is it different than your experiences in the past? How?

_____

_____

_____

Which part of your worship time seemed to draw you nearest to the heart of God?

_____

_____

_____

In what way do you believe that closeness made it more possible to discern how He desired you to pray about different issues?

_____

_____

_____

Describe the difference in what you thought you might pray versus the way God led you to pray.

_____

_____

_____

Explain the wisdom you see in the way God asked you to pray.

_____

_____

_____

And He who searches the hearts knows what the mind of the Spirit is, because He makes intercession for the saints according to the will of God.

ROMANS 8:27 (*NKJV*)

A Personal Prayer

Date: _____ Time: _____

_____

_____

_____

_____

_____

_____

_____

_____

_____

_____

_____

_____

_____

_____

_____

_____

_____

DAY EIGHT

Because God inhabits the praises of His people, few things will draw Him nearer than our praise and worship. He delights in teaching us different ways of worshiping Him so that our time together might be filled with His creative touch.

Before you pray, worship the Father. Then after your time of worship, describe how the Father has asked you to worship Him today.

_____

_____

_____

_____

_____

Explain how this may be different from other ways you have worshiped Him.

_____

_____

_____

_____

_____

List three ways your heart has responded to meeting with Him in "His way" for your time together.

1. _____

_____

2. _____

_____

3. _____

_____

Do you experience His presence more readily in a creative way of prayer and worship? Explain.

_____

_____

_____

Every record you keep of the ways God speaks to you will minister to you in the months and years to come. Don't forget to write them down.

But You are Holy,
Enthroned in the praises of Israel.

PSALM 22:3 (NKJV)

A Personal Prayer

Date: _____ Time: _____

_____

_____

_____

_____

_____

_____

_____

_____

_____

_____

_____

_____

_____

_____

DAY NINE

Perhaps one of the biggest surprises comes when
the Lord simply asks you to sit and be still. He just
wants to be with you. He isn't interested in words;
He just wants you to let Him love you.

Describe how it felt when the Lord asked this of you. If it has not yet
happened, ask Him to bring you into this new intimacy.

_____

_____

_____

_____

_____

List three things that make "just sitting" more difficult than it appears to be.

1. _____

_____

2. _____

_____

3. _____

_____

Explain your response after such a "just sitting" time with Him.

_____

_____

_____

How did He reveal Himself to you during those moments?

_____

_____

_____

Take a moment to thank God for His desire to calm your heart and simply love you in such a sweet way.

_____

_____

_____

Be sure to write down any special ways God directs you to pray and any way in which He speaks to your spirit.

Be still and know that I am God . . .

PSALM 46:10 (*NKJV*)

A Personal Prayer

Date: _____ Time: _____

_____

_____

_____

_____

_____

_____

_____

_____

_____

_____

_____

_____

_____

_____

W e must be willing to sing in our quiet times no matter what the sound . . . for God delights in the songs of our hearts, especially when they are songs of worship.

God waits for us to put away our insecurities and self–consciousness so that we can come to Him as a child. Remember, He is the one who said: "I tell you the truth; anyone who will not receive the kingdom of God like a little child will never enter it" (Mark 10:15 NIV). Our God seeks those who will come into His presence with open hands, an open heart, and a desire to please Him no matter what He might ask. This is a heart ready to worship and ready to pray.

—from *The Heart of Prayer*, chapter 2

DAY TEN

Some of your times with God might start by making up a song about Him or singing of His wonderful creative power, His beauty, or His faithfulness. You're His child—feel free to express your delight in Him through a simple childlike song.

List several ways the Lord has called you to worship Him in uncomplicated, childlike ways.

1. _____

_____

2. _____

_____

3. _____

_____

Explain any reservations you might have felt going into such an experience.

_____

_____

_____

_____

_____

Describe the connection you felt with God's heart when you were obedient to humble yourself like a child and approach Him like that.

_____

_____

_____

Express how you felt, and how it might have affected your entire prayer time.

_____

_____

_____

Ask the Lord to keep your heart tender and open, like that of child, in your future times of worship and prayer.

_____

_____

_____

Be sure to journal all the Lord speaks to your spirit as you seek conversational prayer with Him.

I will praise the name of God with a song,
And will magnify Him with thanksgiving.

PSALM 69:30 (NKJV)

A Personal Prayer

Date: _____ Time: _____

_____

_____

_____

_____

_____

_____

_____

_____

_____

_____

_____

_____

_____

_____

DAY ELEVEN

To worship the Father before we pray brings Him
great joy, but to live a life of worship prepares
us for the prayers of a lifetime!

What does the term "becoming worship" mean to you personally? What part of becoming worship might be the most life–changing for you?

_____

_____

_____

List four ways in which you believe you are growing toward becoming worship.

1. _____

_____

2. _____

_____

3. _____

_____

4. _____

_____

Now list ways you would like the Lord to strengthen you in ways you hadn't even considered might be a part of becoming worship.

_____

_____

_____

In the past, what avenues of worship have been the most difficult for you? Ask the Lord how He would have you pray about these.

_____

_____

_____

It is important for you to record the ways God calls you to worship and pray, as well as what He may speak to your spirit during your conversational prayer times.

For we are the circumcision,
who worship God in the Spirit,
rejoice in Christ Jesus, and have
no confidence in the flesh.

PHILIPPIANS 3:3 *(NKJV)*

A Personal Prayer

Date: _____ Time: _____

_____

_____

_____

_____

_____

_____

_____

_____

_____

_____

_____

_____

_____

_____

_____

_____

_____

_____

_____

DAY TWELVE

*Perhaps one of the greatest purposes of prayer
is to keep us constantly connected to our God.
He knows us, and He desires us to know Him.*

Describe how you feel when you have not been able to have your "set aside" time with the Lord because of life's interruptions.

_____

_____

_____

Explain any way you believe that missed time has affected your day.

_____

_____

_____

List three ways your confidence or strength may have been affected by missing that special time with the Lord.

1. _____

_____

2. _____

_____

3. _____

_____

Chronicle any feelings of loss or disconnection that come when you are not able to be with the Lord in prayer for several days, or longer.

_____

_____

_____

_____

Now describe the difference you feel when you've been with Him.

_____

_____

_____

_____

Remember to keep a record of the ways God directs you in prayer and of any personal responses He may give when you listen for His voice.

And this is eternal life, that they may know You,
the only true God, and Jesus Christ whom You have sent.

JOHN 17:3 (NKJV)

A Personal Prayer

Date: _____ Time: _____

_____

_____

_____

_____

_____

_____

_____

_____

_____

_____

_____

_____

_____

_____

_____

_____

_____

_____

DAY THIRTEEN

*God wants us to accept all of who He is. He desires
us to enjoy Him for the good things, as well as the things
He lets touch our lives that we don't understand.*

List three of the hardest things for you to accept about God's ways.

1. _____

   _____

2. _____

   _____

3. _____

   _____

Is it more difficult for you to love Him when you think of those certain things you've listed?

_____

_____

_____

_____

_____

_____

_____

How important is it for you to be completely accepted by others, even though others might not understand all of your ways? Can you admit that longing in your own heart?

_____

_____

_____

_____

Ask the Lord to take you to a place where you trust His heart so completely that you are ready to love and accept Him for all that He is and all that He allows. Be sure to write your prayer on the pages that follow.

_____

_____

_____

_____

Shall we indeed accept good from God,
and shall we not accept adversity?

JOB 2:10 *(NKJV)*

A Personal Prayer

Date: _____ Time: _____

_____

_____

_____

_____

_____

_____

_____

_____

_____

_____

_____

_____

_____

_____

_____

_____

I t wasn't difficult to love God when my life was in order, but could I continue to love a God who would allow terrible things to happen? Could I say, "Shall we accept good from God, and not trouble?" (Job 2:10 NIV).

. . . I've come to rest more and more in the knowledge that my God is in control and reigns over all things, whether it be the peace we feel or the storm that rages about us. Accepting it has brought me into a far more intimate relationship with Him. Only those who come to relate to Him and trust Him based upon His sovereignty are able to receive all of God—Lord over the good things and Lord over the painful things of life.

—from *The Heart of Prayer*, chapter 3

*Relating to God isn't just accepting everything about Him;
it also means we are willing to spend time with Him. How
can a friendship grow if we don't take time to be together?
And how shall we know what He desires of us if we
don't talk with Him and listen to His heart?*

List three ways you try to spend quality time with the Lord either in a "set
aside" time and/or moments throughout the day.

1. _____

_____

2. _____

_____

3. _____

_____

Describe the difference in the closeness you feel to Him when you
experience these times on a consistent basis.

_____

_____

_____

_____

Describe the difference you see between those times when you pray without listening for God to speak and when you patiently wait to hear His desire for you in prayer and devotional time.

_____

_____

_____

Explain ways your faith is empowered as you re–read the words He has spoken to you.

_____

_____

_____

Write everything you believe God is speaking personally to your heart. As the months and years pass, reflecting on His words will renew your heart and lift your faith.

In the morning, O LORD, You hear my voice;
in the morning I lay my requests before
You and wait in expectation.

A Personal Prayer

Date: _____ Time: _____

_____

_____

_____

_____

_____

_____

_____

_____

_____

_____

_____

_____

_____

_____

_____

_____

DAY FIFTEEN

An amazing miracle takes place when you and I pray.
God has ordained that He will accomplish much upon
this earth through the prayers of His people.
He has a plan, and has chosen those who
will partner with Him to bring forth
that plan through prayer.

Explain a recent prayer that, when answered, assured you that God placed that prayer in your heart and then brought an answer according to His higher plan.

_____

_____

_____

_____

Describe what it means to you personally to be in partnership with God in accomplishing His purposes.

_____

_____

_____

_____

Describe three miracles you believe have come as a result of prayer.

1. _____

_____

2. _____

_____

3. _____

_____

Like a child, try to imagine what it's like to walk beside the Father in partnership while He brings all things to pass regarding His kingdom on earth. Ask the Father to give you a picture of that hand–in–hand undertaking. What do you see?

_____

_____

_____

Every record you keep of the ways God speaks to you will minister to you in the months and years to come. Don't forget to write them down.

His intent was that now, through the church,
the manifold wisdom of God should be made known
to the rulers and authorities in the heavenly realms,
according to His eternal purpose which He
accomplished in Christ Jesus our Lord.

EPHESIANS 3:10, 11 (NIV)

A Personal Prayer

Date: _____ Time: _____

_____

_____

_____

_____

_____

_____

_____

_____

_____

_____

_____

_____

_____

_____

_____

_____

_____

_____

_____

_____

❦ DAY SIXTEEN ❧

We need to be honest with our Father. One truly honest prayer might be, "Lord, I don't even know how to really long for You and Your ways. Please teach me."

Do you believe you can be completely honest with God in prayer? Do you tell Him how you really feel even when you are angry with Him?

_____

_____

_____

After Job expressed his anger toward God, God responded to Job by explaining His sovereignty. Did He punish Job for being honest about his anger? Will He punish you if He did not punish Job?

_____

_____

_____

Describe your present state regarding your desire to know God and to understand His ways.

_____

_____

_____

Have you ever been filled with a longing to truly know God?

_____

_____

_____

Do you desire to grow in that longing for and knowledge of God as you
walk out your spiritual journey?

_____

_____

_____

Ask the Lord to draw you more deeply into that place of longing. Understand
that with longing there will always be some pain, for our longings will not be
fulfilled completely until we enter His heavenly kingdom.

_____

_____

_____

Now journal your prayer time, especially any way in which the Lord
speaks to your heart about His sovereignty or His ways in your life.

One thing I have desired of the of the LORD, that I will seek:
That I may dwell in the house of the LORD all the days of my life,
To behold the beauty of the LORD,
And to inquire in His temple.

PSALM 27:4 *(NKJV)*

A Personal Prayer

Date: _____ Time: _____

_____

_____

_____

_____

_____

_____

_____

_____

_____

_____

_____

_____

_____

_____

_____

The most exciting part of partnering with God in prayer is realizing that the God of the universe desires to move hand–in–hand with frail human beings in carrying out His plans on earth. I don't know about you, but that idea takes my breath away. What are we human beings that He should give us such a privilege? What a wonder!

"What is man, that You should exalt him, that You should set your heart upon him, that you should visit him every morning?"

JOB 7:17,18 (NKJV)

DAY SEVENTEEN

Let's look at spiritual passion—the fervent desire for God and the things that please Him.

Explain what you have believed passion to be in the past.

_____

_____

_____

_____

Describe what spiritual passion feels like . . . or the way it seems to express itself in your life.

_____

_____

_____

_____

Explain how differently you function when you experience that passion or passionate longing.

_____

_____

_____

_____

When you do not experience that passion or longing?

_____

_____

_____

_____

Describe how others respond when they sense a spiritual passion coming from you.

_____

_____

_____

_____

Be sure to write down any special ways God directs you to pray and any way in which He speaks to you.

As the deer pants for streams of water,
so my soul pants for You, O God.

PSALM 42:1 *(NIV)*

A Personal Prayer

Date: _____ Time: _____

_____

_____

_____

_____

_____

_____

_____

_____

_____

_____

_____

_____

_____

_____

_____

_____

_____

_____

DAY EIGHTEEN

Passion is important to our prayer life. Passion is full of life and energy and is fully alive to the moment.

Explain how you personally feel "more alive" to Him during your prayer time when you are experiencing spiritual passion.

_____

_____

_____

Does the life you experience through spiritual passion touch the lives of others?

_____

_____

_____

Describe the difference you feel when that passion or longing is waning.

_____

_____

_____

_____

_____

How does the loss of passion affect your times in prayer?

_____

_____

_____

List three ways passion invigorates or brings life to your walk with the Lord.

1. _____

_____

2. _____

_____

3. _____

_____

Continue to record the ways God speaks to your heart and any special ways He may call you to worship Him.

For Your love is better than wine . . .
Draw me after You and let us run together!

SONG OF SOLOMON 1:2, 4 *(NAS)*

A Personal Prayer

Date: _____ Time: _____

_____

_____

_____

_____

_____

_____

_____

_____

_____

_____

_____

_____

_____

_____

_____

_____

_____

_____

_____

_____

_____

"*I write to you, little children, because your sins are forgiven you for His name's sake. I write to you, fathers, because you have known Him who is from the beginning. I write to you, young men, because you have overcome the wicked one*" (1 John 2:12,13 NKJV).

I believe that we can apply this principle to prayer. We have the little ones, the immature who beg and plead like a child in prayer. In prayer, the young men represent those who have come to know the power and privileges of belonging to God. They see the power of prayer. They are the doers.

The fathers, however, are those who know God. In prayer, the fathers are those who have become one with God's sovereignty and have fallen deeply in love with Him. Their prayers are a time of sweetness, intimacy, friendship, listening for His voice, and resting in His love that purposes all things. This is maturity in prayer—knowing Him.

Our heart's desire is to attain fatherhood (or motherhood!) in prayer as we grow toward becoming the heart of God in prayer.

—from *The Heart of Prayer*, chapter 4

DAY NINETEEN

Our heart's desire is to attain "fatherhood" in prayer as we grow. The "fathers" of whom we speak are the mature believers who pray from a position of rest (1 John 2:12,13). They are aware of God being in control of all things, certain that He loves them, and are totally convinced that He always chooses the highest good.

List three things that you believe have kept you from the rest that can be found in prayer.

1. _____

_____

2. _____

_____

3. _____

_____

Describe three steps you can take to remove these hindrances to a peaceful and restful prayer time.

1. _____

_____

2. _____

_____

3. _____

_____

If attaining "fatherhood" in prayer means we are fully convinced that:

1. God is in control of all things
2. God loves us
3. God always chooses the highest good

then expound on what each one of these assurances means to you personally. (Give personal examples.)

_____

_____

_____

Remember to record the ways God directs you in prayer and of any personal responses He may give when you listen for His voice.

The mind of man plans his way,
But the LORD directs his steps.

PROVERBS 16:9 (NAS)

For the Father Himself loves you . . .

JOHN 16:27 (NAS)

. . . Those who seek the LORD lack no good thing.

PSALM 34:10 (NIV)

A Personal Prayer

Date: _____ Time: _____

_____

_____

_____

_____

_____

_____

_____

_____

_____

_____

_____

_____

_____

_____

_____

_____

_____

_____

_____

I magine sharing your heart with someone you love. You start by telling them how much you love them, you express your joy at all the wonderful things they have brought to your life, and you continue by sharing your intimate longings and struggles. You have opened your heart to this dear friend—even your desire to be a better friend— but in response to all you have said there is nothing but silence. After awhile you leave that place of meeting, but something is missing. The one you love says nothing.

Most of my early years of walking with Christ seem much like the one you just read. I was never told that God wanted to converse with me and that He actually would speak in the stillness of my heart. But now I know how He delights in speaking into our thoughts, for He desires a genuine inter- change with us.

—from *The Heart of Prayer*, chapter 5

DAY TWENTY

Listening to God begins with believing that He desires to speak to you and that given a chance, He will.

List any reasons why you believe the Lord might want to communicate with you personally.

_____

_____

_____

_____

List any misgivings you might have about personally hearing God's voice.

_____

_____

_____

_____

Describe your desire for Him to speak to you in spite of your misgivings.

_____

_____

_____

_____

Ask God's forgiveness for any way you have limited Him in the past, and ask for a heart that is open to any new way He may choose to speak to your heart.

_____

_____

_____

_____

_____

_____

_____

_____

_____

It is important for you to record the ways God calls you to worship and pray, as well as what He may speak to your heart during your conversational prayer times.

He shall call upon Me, and I will answer him . . .

PSALM 91:15 (*NKJV*)

A Personal Prayer

Date: _____ Time: _____

_____

_____

_____

_____

_____

_____

_____

_____

_____

_____

_____

_____

_____

_____

_____

_____

_____

_____

_____

Personal Listening Prayer

There is exceeding power in the prayers of one who seeks God's way . . . who seeks the desire of God in prayer. Eternally, those who consistently ask for His good, His will, and His way in prayer will never be disappointed.

As intercessor/chaplain for the speakers and staff of Women of Faith Conferences, I dedicate every Friday to praying for the conference, doing spiritual battle for an open heaven, asking for God's Word for the staff, and then walking and claiming the stage as God's rightful throne for the weekend—the place from which He will speak to His people. To simply ask Him to bless the gathering and all who come is not enough. He has made it clear that I am to come to Him asking how He would have me pray. I especially remember doing that very thing when Women of Faith conferences traveled to Atlanta in July 2000. These were my words:

> *Father,*
> *Show me how to pray for this staff. I have no words and I am not interested in just words. They mean little in prayer. You are interested in hearts. Teach me how to pray Your heart and Your power for these who will stand before such a great people. How shall I pray for those who speak, who sing, and who lead?"*

His response to my spirit was:

My Child,
Calvary was My passion to pour out mercy . . . to pay for
and supply the needs of the sick and the lost . . . to speak
life into your death. My Son conquered the world, the flesh,
and the devil, by utter submission to need nothing but Me;
nothing but God.

I long for you, My children, to come to that same complete
submission that needs nothing but Me, for out of that
submission is born in You My very heart. Not a human
heart, but the heart of a God that pours out mercy and
loving kindness with an ardent desire for good toward every
soul it touches.

I long for you to be My passion to pour out mercy. I desire to
make you the very heartbeat of the cross . . . and then by My
Spirit to pour you out on this great people who are waiting
for My touch.

And my heart responded back to His:

O Father,
Let it be so in each one of us. Teach us the depths of the
meaning of Your Word, for we long to walk in it. Bring Your
Word to pass in us for Your great glory. Now, hide those who
deliver Your message this weekend. Gather, in the humility of

the person of Jesus, and send them forth—both singers and speakers—to minister with angels, and to call forth Your kingdom in this hour, in this place.

Great and wonderful is our God who draws life from death, and mighty is He who goes before us to perform His Word among us.

All honor and power and glory be unto You and to the Lamb forever and ever.
Amen

These were the words the Lord placed in my heart in answer to the question, "How shall I pray Your Heart?"

*To wait upon
the Lord
is the perfection
of activity.*

OSWALD CHAMBERS

❧ DAY TWENTY·ONE ❧

One day as I was praying, I felt the Lord saying to me, "Try Me.
Just try Me." I knew He was talking about personal listening
prayer. I had grown to desire this kind of interchange so
badly that I finally was ready to risk being wrong.

Describe what you believe to be the biggest risks of personal listening prayer.

_____

_____

_____

Do you believe it is worth the risk to experience God speaking to you in this way? Explain.

_____

_____

_____

Explain the ways in which the Lord seems to be saying, "Try Me. Just try Me," to you.

_____

_____

_____

Explain what you hope to see as a result of having listening prayer in your spiritual life.

_____

_____

_____

Seek the Lord in prayer, asking Him to give you the courage to face any fears you may have of coming to Him in listening prayer.

_____

_____

_____

Remember to keep a record of the ways God directs you in prayer and of any personal responses He may give when you listen for His voice.

> *To the LORD I cry aloud, and He answers me from His holy hill.*
>
> PSALM 3:4 (*NIV*)

A Personal Prayer

Date: _____ Time: _____

_____

_____

_____

_____

_____

_____

_____

_____

_____

_____

_____

_____

_____

_____

One of my very first prayers as a believer in Christ was that God would speak to me face–to–face, like a man speaks to his friend—the way He spoke to Moses in Exodus 33:11. However, my fear of "not doing it right" kept me paralyzed for some time. What if I made it up? Why would God speak to someone like me? Fear. Fear. Fear!

The veil of separation between God and man was destroyed at the crucifixion; the Father now calls us to come freely into His presence. With this in mind, I began to think, "Perhaps hearing Him speak might now be possible for all of His children."

—from *The Heart of Prayer,* chapter 5

DAY TWENTY·TWO

*God loves to speak to His people, and what He says may
be expressed differently to each person. He uses human hearts
to write His words so that what we hear will be fashioned through
the grid of our own personality and ways of expression. He
will speak if we will only risk asking and waiting on Him.*

As you read the Gospels, can you discern how the writers expressed themselves differently even though they saw and experienced the same things
and heard the same words from Christ? What does this say to you?

_____

_____

_____

_____

Describe any insecurity you may feel when you hear about how others hear
from God.

_____

_____

_____

_____

Are you willing to let the Lord speak through your own way of expressing yourself? Do the words need to sound like words others write when they hear God?

_____

_____

_____

Ask the Lord to help you allow Him to speak through you in unique, individual ways. (Never compare your conversations with God to how others communicate with Him.)

_____

_____

_____

Remember to keep a record of the ways God directs you in prayer and of any personal responses He may give when you listen for His voice.

Whether you turn to the right or to the left,
your ears will hear a voice behind you,
saying, "This is the way; walk in it."

ISAIAH 30:21 (*NIV*)

A Personal Prayer

Date: _____ Time: _____

_____
_____
_____
_____
_____
_____
_____
_____
_____
_____
_____
_____
_____
_____
_____
_____
_____

DAY TWENTY·THREE

he world's way is to hound someone until we receive what we want or need. Jesus describes the Father's way: "Simply ask and it will be given to you. Seek and you shall find. Knock and it will be opened to you."

List three prayers you have prayed and believed God would answer without your returning to Him again and again with the same requests.

1. _____

_____

2. _____

_____

3. _____

_____

List three prayers that you have prayed many times.

1. _____

_____

2. _____

_____

3. _____

_____

If you believe God is leading you to pray again and again over the same issue, explain why you believe this might be the case.

_____

_____

_____

Describe any continued prayers that might have been emotionally motivated rather than motivated by God's desire for prayer.

_____

_____

_____

Be sure to journal any way that God speaks to you during your prayer time today.

Ask, and it will be given to you;
seek, and you will find;
knock, and it will be opened to you.
For everyone who asks receives,
and he who seeks finds,
and to him who knocks
it will be opened.

MATTHEW 7:7,8 (NKJV)

A Personal Prayer

Date: _____ Time: _____

_____

_____

_____

_____

_____

_____

_____

_____

_____

_____

_____

_____

_____

_____

_____

*T*hen [the angel] said to me, "Do not be afraid, Daniel, for from the first day that you set your heart on understanding . . . and on humbling yourself before your God, your words were heard, and I have come in response to your words" (Daniel 10:12 NAS).

In this passage, God teaches us two very clear principles of prayer. The first is that answered prayer often comes as a result of our desire to understand, and the second is our willingness to humble ourselves before God.

—from *The Heart of Prayer*, chapter 6

DAY TWENTY·FOUR

A prayerful heart is always willing for God to reveal issues
of pride or disobedience in order that we might ask forgiveness and
once again be restored to that sweet relationship for which our heart yearns.

Explain why you believe it is important to have a heart–cleansing before
prayer time.

_____

_____

_____

List any areas of confession that came as a surprise during your prayer time
today. (Something God showed you that you were not aware of.)

_____

_____

_____

Describe how you have felt in the past when you have not quickly confessed
to God those ways you have fallen short of His great love for you.

_____

_____

_____

What differences do you experience in your walk with the Lord when you have neglected to seek a cleansed heart over a period of time?

_____

_____

_____

_____

_____

_____

It is important not to become legalistic about asking God's forgiveness for our sins. Remember, if we ask, He forgives. He has given His Word. There is a consistent experience of relief and release when we ask for cleansing as a part of our daily time with the Lord.

Journal all communication that takes place between you and the Lord during your time with Him. These records will be meaningful to you in the days and years to come.

Create in me a clean heart, O God,
And renew a steadfast spirit within me.

PSALM 51:10 *(NKJV)*

A Personal Prayer

Date: _____ Time: _____

_____
_____
_____
_____
_____
_____
_____
_____
_____
_____
_____
_____
_____
_____
_____
_____
_____
_____
_____

The key to victory over wandering thoughts is not to give up.
We must not walk away from our times with the Lord
because of the battle to discipline our minds.
Rather, we must work through it.

List the types of thoughts that invade your prayer time.

1. _____

   _____

2. _____

   _____

3. _____

   _____

4. _____

   _____

5. _____

   _____

Describe the ways you have tried to deal with these distractions.

_____

_____

_____

What successes or failures have you experienced?

_____

_____

_____

Describe four ways you will try to resolves these types of interference.

1. _____

   _____

2. _____

   _____

3. _____

   _____

4. _____

   _____

Don't forget to journal your conversation with the Lord today. Keeping a record of His words to you are an important part of your time with Him.

God is in the midst of her, she shall not be moved; God shall help her . . .

PSALM 46:5 *(NKJV)*

A Personal Prayer

Date: _____ Time: _____

_____
_____
_____
_____
_____
_____
_____
_____
_____
_____
_____
_____
_____
_____
_____
_____
_____
_____
_____
_____
_____

When stray thoughts interfere with my prayers, I quickly remind the enemy that my God is patient and kind and filled with understanding for my wandering mind. I acknowledge this as yet another opportunity to praise my Father. Our adversary doesn't like to be a facilitator of praise for his holy Opponent. My words of praise sting and cause him to pause his efforts to disrupt. However, if the battle continues, I have found that pausing to sing a short song to the Lord helps to refocus my mind and draw me right back into His presence.

—from *The Heart of Prayer*, chapter 6

DAY TWENTY·SIX

Remember the battle is for the mind. We give it to the Lord in prayer and we ask Him to protect it. A distracted prayer is not a reason to "beat ourselves up" because we don't think we are doing it right. Rather, it is an opportunity to thank God for how graciously He accepts us even in our weaknesses, and how quickly He forgives and shows us ways to draw near to Him in prayer.

In what ways have you demeaned yourself because you struggle with a wandering mind as it relates to prayer?

_____

_____

_____

What new messages now replace the old ones?

_____

_____

_____

Has the Lord shown you other ways to win the battle for the mind other than those you have learned through *The Heart of Prayer* or another prayer book? List those below.

_____

_____

_____

How has your attitude toward prayer changing as you gain more control over your wandering thoughts?

_____

_____

_____

Be sure to record any way the Lord may speak to you during your prayer time. Also, write down any thoughts that come to you as a result of asking Him how He would have you pray.

When my anxious thoughts multiply within me,
Your consolations delight my soul.

PSALM 94:19 *(NAS)*

A Personal Prayer

Date: _____ Time: _____

_____

_____

_____

_____

_____

_____

_____

_____

_____

_____

_____

_____

_____

_____

DAY TWENTY·SEVEN

Believing God's Word is vital to the foundation you need
to pray effectively. We must trust that the God who spoke the
Word loves us, desires only our very best, and will not grant
the desired answer if doing so will be destructive to us somehow.

List three prayers that you believe might not have been answered the way
you desired because the answer could have been destructive to you in the
future.

1. _____

_____

2. _____

_____

3. _____

_____

God's Word tells us that He loves us with an everlasting love and that His
love is unconditional. Do you struggle with believing this could really be
true? In what ways?

_____

_____

_____

_____

How do you think these struggles might affect your prayer life?

_____

_____

_____

_____

_____

Do you believe that God wants your very best? What about those times when your desires conflict with what He knows to be best? Are you able to rest in God's sovereignty during those times? Describe.

_____

_____

_____

_____

_____

Express your desires for any needed change of heart as you pray today. Write down your conversation with the Father and any words He may impress upon your heart.

The testimony of the LORD is sure,
making wise the simple.

PSALM 19:7 *(NKJV)*

A Personal Prayer

Date: _____ Time: _____

_____
_____
_____
_____
_____
_____
_____
_____
_____
_____
_____
_____
_____
_____
_____
_____

God takes all things into consideration. For instance, when you pray for a friend or loved one, He considers whether your request, when answered, would be the highest good for you, for the person for whom you are praying, and for all others involved. He carefully weaves all of these motivations together to produce the right answer at the most timely moment.

All of this takes us back to the sovereignty of God. Do we want His absolute best? Do we believe those things he has spoken are really true?

—from *The Heart of Prayer*, chapter 7

❧ DAY TWENTY·EIGHT ❧

". . . Nevertheless, not as I will, but as You will."

MATTHEW 26:39 (*NKJV*)

Jesus' prayer recorded in Matthew 26:39 is from the Son to the Father. It is every bit God's prayer to God. In the very heart of prayer, we find God's prayer, and in God's prayer we will never be disillusioned.

Describe a prayer that you believe might have come from the heart of God. It could be a prayer you never would have imagined praying.

_____

_____

_____

How did this prayer seem different from other prayers?

_____

_____

_____

Describe the peace you felt in knowing you were praying just as God was directing you to pray.

_____

_____

_____

What is your heart's desire regarding future maturity in praying the heart of God?

_____

_____

_____

Remember, maturing in this type of prayer takes time. At first, you will not feel that you are praying God's heart about every prayer request. Be patient. Growing is a process, and the Father delights to guide His children through this journey.

O My Father, if it is possible,
let this cup pass from Me; nevertheless,
not as I will, but as You will.

MATTHEW 26:39 (*NKJV*)

A Personal Prayer

Date: _____ Time: _____

_____

_____

_____

_____

_____

_____

_____

_____

_____

_____

_____

_____

_____

_____

DAY TWENTY·NINE

Although God might not instantly make us aware of His heart on a particular matter, as we meditate during the days or weeks that follow, light often will be given regarding how we should pray for that situation or person. Until we know His heart, we can pray as our heart leads, while always remaining open to His changing the focus of our prayer.

Describe a time when you sought God's heart in prayer and felt you didn't receive an answer.

_____

_____

_____

_____

_____

Did you ask Him to talk to you about the situation or person in the days that follow? If your answer is, "No," ask Him now.

_____

_____

_____

_____

_____

How did you eventually come to understand that you were to pray about the matter?

_____

_____

_____

_____

_____

Describe the difference between how you initially prayed and then the way God told you to pray. Can you see God's wisdom in asking you to pray as He did? Explain.

_____

_____

_____

_____

_____

Be sure to journal God's words to you. These will be important insights for you to read over again and again through the years.

Father, glorify Your name.

JOHN 12:28 (*NKJV*)

A Personal Prayer

Date: _____ Time: _____

_____
_____
_____
_____
_____
_____
_____
_____
_____
_____
_____
_____
_____
_____
_____
_____
_____
_____

DAY THIRTY

The key to all victorious intercession (going to God on another's behalf) is, "Hearing the heart of the Father." Another important aspect of intercessory prayer is our willingness to identify with the problems of the person for whom we pray.

God was willing to identify with us in the form of Jesus, becoming man and living a human life in this world. In that way, Jesus humbled Himself and identified with us before He rose to heaven to intercede for us. No wonder He wants us to be willing to identify with those for whom we pray!

Example:

You might be praying for someone who is a drug addict. Although you might never have experienced such a problem you can identify with the struggle by saying, "Father, so many times I have run to something besides You when I was upset or wanting something I couldn't have. I know what it is like to run the wrong direction to get my needs met, and so my heart goes out to _____, who is imprisoned by her need for those things that can only bring her pain and keep her from You. Lord, You are the only One who can comfort her heart and bring her peace."

Describe a time when you identified with another person's struggles, then lifted them to the Lord in prayer. Describe the way(s) in which you humbled yourself by identifying with that person before the Father.

_____

_____

_____

Why do you believe it is so humbling to identify with another before you pray for them?

_____

_____

_____

What would it indicate about our prayer life if we either refused to or saw no need to identify with those for whom we pray?

_____

_____

_____

Be sure to journal God's words and impressions to you.

Likewise the Spirit also helps in our weaknesses.
For we do not know what we should pray for as we
ought, but the Spirit Himself makes intercession
for us with groanings which cannot be uttered.

ROMANS 8:26 (*NKJV*)

A Personal Prayer

Date: _____ Time: _____

_____
_____
_____
_____
_____
_____
_____
_____
_____
_____
_____
_____
_____
_____
_____
_____
_____
_____
_____
_____

These are the elements we see in the Lord's Prayer: worship, acknowledging God's will as the highest and best, personal requests, asking forgiveness/ cleansing, and seeking protection against evil.

God knows that each of these is important to the human heart because of who we are and because of the world in which we live.

—from *The Heart of Prayer*, chapter 7

DAY THIRTY·ONE

When we ask God how He would have us pray, we are
saying in the simplest way, ". . . nevertheless, not my will
but Thy will be done." Such sweet closure comes to
our heart when we leave the Father's request
with the Father. We are moving into
that place of rest called prayer.

Explain the hardest part of praying, "Not my will but Thy will be done."

_____

_____

_____

_____

_____

If such a prayer frightens you, are you still trusting God's heart? Spend time meditating on His faithfulness to you and the ways that He has proven that you can trust His heart. Describe.

_____

_____

_____

_____

_____

What changes inside of you when you finally can tell Him, "Not my will but Thy will be done?"

_____

_____

_____

If this prayerful surrender is a struggle for you, ask the Father to reveal and heal any wounds that keep you from trusting His heart for you.

_____

_____

_____

Journal your time with the Lord and record any ways that He speaks to your spirit today.

There remains therefore a rest for the people of God.

HEBREWS 4:9 (NKJV)

A Personal Prayer

Date: _____ Time: _____

_____

_____

_____

_____

_____

_____

_____

_____

_____

_____

_____

_____

_____

_____

_____

_____

_____

One of the greatest privileges of prayer is receiving God's answers. Although many answers are clear from the beginning, we have to wait for other answers. And still others may even draw us into the midst of a miracle.

Which answer to prayer is most difficult for you to hear—"Yes," "No," or "Not now"? Explain.

_____

_____

_____

_____

_____

List three prayers that were answered so quickly you could hardly believe it.

1. _____

_____

2. _____

_____

3. _____

_____

List three prayers for which you have been awaiting God's answer over a considerable amount of time.

1. _____

_____

2. _____

_____

3. _____

_____

Describe any answers to prayer that have drawn you into the midst of a miracle (whether a personal prayer or a prayer group in which you were involved).

_____

_____

_____

Be sure to journal any way the Lord speaks to you, even if the communication seems insignificant at the time.

He shall call upon Me,
and I will answer him . . .

PSALM 91:15 (*NKJV*)

A Personal Prayer

Date: _____ Time: _____

_____

_____

_____

_____

_____

_____

_____

_____

_____

_____

_____

_____

_____

_____

_____

_____

I t is important that we not fashion what we think should be the answer to any prayer; it is enough to know that God answers all the prayers of His children.

"The eyes of the Lord are on the righteous, and His ears are open to their cries" (Psalm 34:15 NKJV).

"He shall call upon Me, and I will answer him" (Psalm 91:15 NKJV).

"Until now you have asked nothing in my name. Ask and you will receive" (John 16:24 NKJV).

"And whatever things you ask in prayer, believing, you will receive" (Matthew 21:22 NKJV).

Remember, for some the answer may be, "Not yet My child," or "It would not be wisdom for Me to give this to you." For others, a response from God might simply be, "Yes." Whichever the case may be, we can be certain no prayer will go unanswered.

—from *The Heart of Prayer*, chapter 8

❧ DAY THIRTY·THREE ❧

What a privilege! We pray to a loving Father who transforms our prayers into the highest good.

List three prayers where God's answer was greater than your prayer.

Your prayers:

1. _____

    _____

2. _____

    _____

3. _____

    _____

God's answers:

1. _____

    _____

2. _____

    _____

3. _____

    _____

How do you see God's answers as the highest good?

_____

_____

_____

_____

_____

_____

_____

Speak to the Lord about your desire that prayers not be limited to what you ask . . . but to His highest good for all. Confess any ways that you have wanted your will above His will in the past.

Be sure to journal those things the Lord speaks to your heart. These will be treasures in the years to come.

> *Amen, blessing and glory and wisdom and*
> *thanksgiving, and honor and power and might,*
> *be to our God forever and ever. Amen.*

REVELATION 7:12 *(NAS)*

A Personal Prayer

Date: _____ Time: _____

_____

_____

_____

_____

_____

_____

_____

_____

_____

_____

_____

_____

_____

_____

Worship is one of the highest forms of prayer, and when worship permeates our responses to the issues of life, we are becoming worship.

List five ways you are learning to respond with worship in the ordinary moments of life.

1. _____

   _____

2. _____

   _____

3. _____

   _____

4. _____

   _____

5. _____

   _____

List some areas of becoming worship that you have not experienced yet.

_____

_____

_____

Ask the Lord to open your heart to a new realization of His presence and sovereignty in every facet of your whole life so that every response might become worship.

_____

_____

_____

_____

_____

Every journal entry should include any way(s) in which the Lord speaks to you through His Word, to your heart, through thoughts, impressions, and so forth. Keep your journal in a protected place because you will want it to last through the years for the Lord's words to speak to you again and again.

Oh come, let us worship and bow down;
Let us kneel before the LORD our Maker.
For He is our God, And we are the people
of His pasture, and the sheep of His hand.

PSALM 95:6, 7 (NKJV)

A Personal Prayer

Date: _____ Time: _____

_____

_____

_____

_____

_____

_____

_____

_____

_____

_____

_____

_____

_____

_____

C hristians have puzzled and been overwhelmed for years over 1 Thessalonians 5:17:

"Pray without ceasing" (KJV, NKJV, NAS).

"Pray continually" (NIV).

"Pray all the time" (MSG).

Most believers look at this verse and say, "That is impossible. God asks too much." However, as God has drawn me into the prayers of His heart, I have come to believe that it is not only possible, but that praying without ceasing ultimately transforms us into prayer itself.

—from *The Heart of Prayer*, chapter 8

DAY THIRTY·FIVE

Longing for unhindered unity with God is a critical part of becoming prayer. Oneness flows out of our relationship with God, and in that oneness our hearts become more and more aware of God's prayers rather than our own.

Describe the ways you set aside times to be with the Lord.

_____

_____

_____

List things you believe have tried to interfere with your intimate fellowship with Him.

1. _____

_____

2. _____

_____

3. _____

_____

4. _____

_____

Which of these distractions can be rearranged? How can you secure the time you need with God?

_____

_____

_____

_____

_____

_____

_____

Journal any responses the Lord may give you as you pray today.

I do not pray for these alone, but also for those
who will believe in Me through their word; that they
all may be one, as You, Father, are in Me, and I in
You; that they also may be one in Us, that the
world may believe that You sent Me.

J O H N   1 7 : 2 0 , 2 1   *(N K J V)*

A Personal Prayer

Date: _____ Time: _____

_____

_____

_____

_____

_____

_____

_____

_____

_____

_____

_____

_____

_____

_____

_____

_____

_____

*Longing for and seeking oneness with each other and
with our God fosters "becoming prayer," but even
unity is not about new habits or external
patterns. Oneness is about heart–set.*

As a result of your new understanding regarding "becoming prayer," what
steps had you already taken in that direction . . . without even realizing you
had done so.

_____

_____

_____

In what ways would you like to see your life become prayer?

_____

_____

_____

Which part of becoming prayer appears to be the most difficult for you?

_____

_____

_____

Ask the Lord to reveal your heart and the ways you can peacefully move into that place called becoming prayer.

_____

_____

_____

_____

Ask the Lord to show you any hindrances, and pray for His strength to move them out of the way.

_____

_____

_____

_____

Give the Lord time to speak to you after your worship and prayer time today. Journal His words or impressions on your heart.

> *And Jesus said to him, "You shall love*
> *the Lord your God with all your heart,*
> *with all your soul, and with your mind.'*
> *This is the first and great commandment.*
> *And the second is like it: 'You shall*
> *love your neighbor as yourself.'"*

MATTHEW 22:37–39 (NKJV)

A Personal Prayer

Date: _____ Time: _____

_____

_____

_____

_____

_____

_____

_____

_____

_____

_____

_____

_____

_____

_____

_____

While *you* can't make this new, vibrant prayer life happen, you can open your arms and your heart wide, asking the *Father* to bring it to pass. Ask Him for a better way and tell Him that you are willing to put away all the regimented approaches to prayer that have been a part of your past. Humble your heart before Him and ask for that which He longs to give you . . . the transition from just simply saying prayer, to actually becoming prayer. It is a gift He would desire for each one of us. How it pleases Him for us to ask!

—from *The Heart of Prayer*, chapter 8

All God desires for
you to be in this life.

All He knew you would
pray to be in Him.

His promise, "I will
accomplish what
concerns you."

His promise, "I will
complete the work I have
begun in you."

*The main thing
that God asks for
is our attention.*

JIM CYMBALA

DAY THIRTY·SEVEN

*God's sovereignty in our personal lives is like a plate
that was prepared for us before birth, which holds perfectly
measured amounts of joy and sorrow, of happiness and pain,
and of struggle and rest. God knew what would be on our plate,
and He also knew everything we would pray about our relationships
and situations. We grow as we pray for what He desires for us
to be during our life on this earth, and we have confidence in
these two promises: "I will accomplish what concerns you."
And "I will complete the work I have begun in you."*

If this is indeed a picture of God's sovereignty in our lives, how can it
change the way we view our circumstances moment by moment?

_____

_____

_____

_____

What new assurances do we have as we view this possibility?

_____

_____

_____

_____

How could our lives become more peaceful and restful in light of what this picture expresses?

_____

_____

_____

Describe the changes that come to your heart as you view God's sovereignty in this way?

_____

_____

_____

During your prayer time today, ask God to affirm this understanding of His sovereignty and to show you clearly how it applies to your life. Be sure to journal your prayer and any way in which He speaks to you.

"I will accomplish what concerns you."
"I will complete the work I have begun in you."

(PARAPHRASE OF **PSALM 138:8; PHILIPPIANS 1:6**)

A Personal Prayer

Date: _____ Time: _____

_____
_____
_____
_____
_____
_____
_____
_____
_____
_____
_____
_____
_____
_____
_____
_____
_____

Humble your heart before Him and ask for that which
He longs to give you . . . the transition from just simply saying
a prayer, to actually becoming prayer. He desires this gift
for each one of us! How it pleases Him for us to ask!

To become prayer, you must possess a humble heart. In what areas do you lack humility?

_____

_____

_____

List any fears you have regarding praying for a humble heart.

_____

_____

_____

How do those fears line up with what the Lord teaches us about the sovereign plate given to us at birth?

_____

_____

_____

If we do not have to fear that more struggle or suffering could come from praying for humility, what else would keep you from offering such a prayer?

_____

_____

_____

In the Song of Solomon, the maiden (who represents the believer) says to her Beloved (who represents Christ), "Catch the foxes for us, the little foxes that are ruining the vineyards, while our vineyards are in blossom" (Song of Solomon 2:15, NAS).

The maiden realizes that these foxes (areas of compromise or sin) in her life can't be removed by her own efforts, so she asks the only one who can to intervene on her behalf. She opens her heart for her Beloved (Christ) to do the work.

Are you ready to pray that the Lord will work on those areas of your life that lack humility so that your fruit for Him will not be destroyed before it even has a chance to bloom? You can trust His heart with this prayer.

If My people who are called by My Name
will humble themselves, and pray . . .
then I will hear from heaven . . .

2 CHRONICLES 7:14 (NKJV)

A Personal Prayer

Date: _____ Time: _____

_____
_____
_____
_____
_____
_____
_____
_____
_____
_____
_____
_____
_____
_____
_____
_____
_____
_____
_____
_____

DAY THIRTY·NINE

The "unforced rhythms of grace" (Matthew 11:29, MSG)
call us to a life of becoming prayer. Such a life does not require
our hard work, but rather simple openness, a longing heart,
and a desire to enter the place of rest called prayer.

Tell the Lord of your desire to have an open heart. Express to Him that if anything in you is not yet ready for openness, then you want to be made willing to have that openness in your life.

_____

_____

_____

List those ways in the past where you have "striven" rather than rested in prayer.

1. _____

_____

2. _____

_____

3. _____

_____

Express your heart's desire to the Lord about coming into restful prayer.

_____

_____

_____

Describe the communication that took place between your heart and the Lord's during your prayer time today. Explain how you might be experiencing the rest of which He speaks when He says, "Come to Me all of you who labor and are heavy-laden, and I will give you rest." (Matthew 11:28 NKJV)

_____

_____

_____

Are you tired? Worn out? Burned out on religion? Come to Me.
Get away with Me and you'll recover your life. I'll show you how
to take a real rest. Walk with Me and work with Me—watch
how I do it. Learn the unforced rhythms of grace. I won't
lay anything heavy or ill-fitting on you. Keep company
with Me and you'll learn to live freely and lightly.

MATTHEW 11:28-30 (MSG)

A Personal Prayer

Date: _____ Time: _____

_____

_____

_____

_____

_____

_____

_____

_____

_____

_____

_____

_____

_____

_____

_____

_____

_____

_____

_____

Those who have experienced the heart–change of self–abandonment in prayer have stepped into the Lord's call to "take up your cross and follow Me." We don't have to ask the Lord to bring us a cross or go looking for one so we can do as He asked—the cross is already on the plate we were given. The question now becomes, "Will you take it up with a new heart–set and follow Me?"

—from *The Heart of Prayer*, Epilogue

DAY FORTY

*t is easy to fear that abandoning ourselves to the Lord
would bring more pain and suffering. However, the Lord impressed
on me that fully abandoning myself to Him would not bring more pain
or sorrow to my plate, for our willingness to give ourselves totally to Him
does not change what has been placed there. What it does is change
the heart of the person who holds the plate, and a heart
so changed is one He delights to display before men.*

How can it change us to understand that full abandonment will not bring
more pain or suffering to our lives?

_____

_____

_____

The person who holds the plate can become either bitter or more tender
in the things of Christ when trials and struggles come. Describe situations
where you had to work through bitterness after God allowed difficult
circumstances to touch your life.

_____

_____

_____

Explain how receiving these happenings as a part of a loving God's sovereignty could change a heart from bitterness to tenderness.

_____

_____

_____

How can a changed heart make it easier to become prayer?

_____

_____

_____

How might this understanding bring rest to your life, both spiritually and emotionally?

_____

_____

_____

It is so important for you to journal you time in prayer. God's words to you now will continue to minister to you as the years go by.

Your eyes saw my unformed body.
All the days ordained for me
were written in Your book
before one of them came to be.

PSALM 139:16 (*NIV*)

A Personal Prayer

Date: _____ Time: _____

_____

_____

_____

_____

_____

_____

_____

_____

_____

_____

_____

_____

_____

Miracles and wonders
are the ordinary stuff
of God's day.

JAN CARLBERG

CONTINUING THE JOURNEY

If *The Women of Faith Prayer Journal* has been meaningful for you, you also might like:

The Heart of Prayer, by Lana Bateman

Throughout this prayer journal you've read excerpts from the companion book, *The Heart of Prayer.* In it Lana unfolds her own journey deeper into prayer, and she encourages women on beautiful, practical ways to enhance their own prayer lives.

Irrepressible Hope: Devotions to Anchor Your Soul and Buoy Your Spirit, by Patsy Clairmont, Barbara Johnson, Nicole Johnson, Marilyn Meberg, Luci Swindoll, and Thelma Wells

The core team of Women of Faith shares sixty devotions of how irrepressible hope has enriched their lives, strengthened their relationships with the Savior, and kept them afloat when circumstances threatened to pull them under.

Keeping a Princess Heart, by Nicole Johnson

This is a thoughtful exploration of the tension women feel between what they *long for* and what they live with in this not so fairy tale world.

Outrageous Love, by Sheila Walsh

It's an outrageous love that a perfect God would give Himself for us. It's an outrageous life that devotes itself wholly back to God's love. Go ahead . . . Be outrageous!

Women of Faith Mission Statement

Women of Faith wants all women to know God loves them unconditionally, no matter what. The ministry reaches out through motivational, yet moving conferences. Since 1996, more than 2,000,000 women have attended Women of Faith events in dozens of cities across North America.

Women of Faith is a nondenominational women's ministry committed to helping women of all faiths, backgrounds, age groups, and nationalities be set free to a lifestyle of God's grace. Founded specifically to meet the needs to women, Women of Faith is committed to nurturing women spiritually, emotionally, and relationally—whether it be in marriages, friendships, the workplace, or with their children. Our goal is to provide hope and encouragement in all areas of life, especially those that can wear women down and steal their joy and hope.

Women of Faith, which has become America's largest women's conference, exists to deliver great news to women: God loves them, and there are a bunch of girlfriends out there who love them, too! Through laughter, music, dramas, and gut-level, real-life stories about how God has worked through the good and bad of our lives, Women of Faith reminds women that God is crazy about them!

For more information or to register
for a conference, please visit
www.womenoffaith.com

or call **1-888-49-FAITH**

As the sun is full of light,

The ocean full of water,

Heaven full of glory,

So may my heart

be full of Thee.

PURITAN PRAYER